COURTSHIP
SOME PRACTICAL ADVICE

Comprising

COURTSHIP FOR GIRLS
Anon
1936

COURTSHIP
Hubert McEvoy SJ
1957

GOING STEADY
Tony Kirwin
1964

SEX EDUCATION: TRAINING IN CHASTITY
Malcolm Brennan
1974

CATHOLIC TRUTH SOCIETY
PUBLISHERS TO THE HOLY SEE

Real, sincere love
between man and woman,
because it is part of our human
nature, comes from God,
and is a good and holy thing.

Hubert McEvoy (1899-1973) was a Jesuit priest.
Nothing is known about the authors of the other texts.

CTS ONEFIFTIES
Originally published as *Courtship for Girls*, 1936; *Courtship*, 1951 (revised edition, 1957); *Going Steady*, 1964; *Sex Education: Training in Chastity*, 1974.
Published by The Incorporated Catholic Truth Society,
40-46 Harleyford Road, London SE11 5AY
www.ctsbooks.org
All rights reserved.
Copyright © 2017 The Incorporated Catholic Truth Society.
ISBN 978 1 78469 541 5

COURTSHIP FOR GIRLS

AND PRACTICAL INSTRUCTIONS FOR THOSE ABOUT TO BE MARRIED

Anon

COURTSHIP

Anon

Real, sincere love between man and woman, because it is part of our human nature, comes from God, and, if we do not degrade it, is a good and holy thing. The life-long union of marriage to which it leads, and for which it is intended, Christ our Lord has raised to be a Sacrament, which puts love on a supernatural level, gives all the graces necessary for married life, and therefore, if husband and wife act generously to God and to each other, will give them happiness, however great their difficulties may be. They fight their battles together with God.

This being so, and since the future happiness of two people here and in the next world is at stake, it would be difficult to exaggerate the importance of the preparation for marriage called courtship. Let us think first of the period *prior to engagement*.

Before Engagement

A man begins to pay special attention to a girl. It is for her a novel experience, full of thrill and romance, if she likes the man. When this happens, and as soon as possible, she should stop to reflect, asking herself several questions. Does she think the man is serious in his intentions or is she merely a source of amusement to him—someone to take to theatres, dances, and the rest? Does she like this man *only* because he knows how to flatter her vanity?

Does she like him *only* on account of his personal appearance, or *only* because he has a good position? Does she know anything of his character, his religion, his ideas of right and wrong? Does she remember that his exterior qualities may cloak a character that may be very good, but may also be bad or weak?

The girl should answer these questions honestly and, if she is doubtful on some point, then her first object must be to get to know the man better. For when he proposes to her, if she does not know the real worth of the man she accepts, she may regret it all her days. Moreover, once she realises that, however attractive she may find the man, he is not likely to make her a good husband, she cannot do better than make clear to him at once that she will never marry him; the pain this may cause both of them is small compared with what both will have to suffer if they rush into marriage without really knowing one another or appreciating the step they are taking.

Before and after Engagement

Both *before and after engagement,* that is to say, during the whole period of courtship up to her wedding-day, it will be well if a girl is fore-armed against some very real dangers. If she will observe the following rules, not only will she keep from sin, and so please God, but she will be taking the best means to make the time of courting one of the happiest in their lives for both herself and the man who is courting her, and she will lay the foundation of one of God's best gifts—a happy married life.

Three Rules

1. The way in which her lover treats her rests for the most part with herself. It is the girl who draws the line and says: "Thus

far, but no farther." If she knows where to stop his advances she will increase his respect for her—if he is the kind of man worth marrying—and in addition she will help him to keep from sin. Let her realise that a pure and holy courtship is the first and most certain condition of a happy married life.

2. Therefore a girl will remember that she may not give a man before marriage all that is rightly his in marriage. At all costs she will keep her modesty, and strictly forbid any action that will tarnish it. Let her be convinced that though previously she has never fallen into sin in this matter, and has always had a horror of it, she may find the temptation far greater than she would have thought possible and, if she is not on her guard, commit sin, mortal sin.

3. At the same time she will be sensible and not go to the other extreme of forbidding the ordinary and honourable signs of love—ordinary kissing and embracing. These are allowed to the engaged. If she loves the man she need not be afraid to show her love in this way.

To keep these rules at a time when all idea of the sanctity of marriage and respect for women has to a great extent disappeared, and when the worst passions are disguised under the name of "love," will not always be easy. Therefore in choosing her future husband, and to strengthen her to keep loyal to God and her conscience, she will get all the assistance possible.

How to Obtain Assistance

1. First and foremost, frequent Confession and Holy Communion, and fidelity to all her religious duties; she will ask our Blessed Lady's help especially. Let the man join her at Mass and Communion, if at all possible; for if he cannot sympathise

with his future wife's desire to serve God he is not fit to be her husband.

2. If she has doubts, difficulties of any kind, she will not think they are new and unheard of, for they are certainly not. Therefore she will be sensible and ask the advice of her confessor, who will understand and be able to guide her.

3. Though girls often find it difficult in these days to believe that their parents may be better judges of a man than they are themselves, yet this is often so. A sensible girl will bring a man who has begun to court her to her own home from the beginning; she will be quite open with her parents about all she does and, if they are good parents, she will never regret following their advice.

4. Finally, let her read over and weigh the words of the present Pope in his "Letter on Christian Marriage" (1930):—[1] "To the proximate preparation of a good married life belongs very especially the care in choosing a partner; on that depends a great deal whether the forthcoming marriage will be happy or not, since one may be to the other either a great help in leading a Christian life, or a great danger and hindrance. And so that they may not deplore for the rest of their lives the sorrows arising from an indiscreet marriage, those about to enter wedlock should carefully deliberate in choosing the person with whom henceforward they must live continually; they should, in so deliberating, keep before their minds the thought first of God and of the true religion of Christ, then of themselves, of their partner, of the children to come, as also of human and civil society, for which wedlock is a fountain head.

"Let them diligently pray for divine help, so that they may make their choice in accordance with Christian prudence,

---
[1] Christian Marriage (The Encyclical *Casti Connubii*), C.T.S, 2d.

not indeed led by the blind and unrestrained impulse of lust, nor by any desire of riches or other base influence, but by a true and noble love, and by a sincere affection for the future partner; and then let them strive in their married life for those ends for which the state was constituted by God.

"Lastly, let them not omit to ask the prudent advice of their parents with regard to the partner, and let them regard this advice in no light manner in order that by their mature knowledge, and experience of human affairs they may guard against a disastrous choice, and on the threshold of matrimony may receive more abundantly the divine blessing of the Fourth Commandment: *Honour thy father and thy mother* which is the first commandment with a promise: *That it may be well with thee and thou mayest be long-lived upon the earth* (Ephes. vi. 2-3)."

PRACTICAL INSTRUCTIONS FOR THOSE ABOUT TO BE MARRIED

(A summary only can here be given. The parish priest will give further details where necessary.)

1. Place of Marriage

The general law of the Church has been in force in England since Easter, 1908, according to which only those marriages, with certain specified exceptions, are valid between Catholics, or between a Catholic and a non-Catholic, which are contracted in the presence of the bishop in his diocese or the parish priest in his parish, or in the presence of priests delegated by them.

The marriage should regularly be celebrated in the parish church of the bride, but for a just cause it may take place in the parish church of the bridegroom. If it be desired that the marriage be celebrated elsewhere, the permission of the parish priest of the parties is required.

2. Banns of Marriage

These are given out for three consecutive Sundays or holydays in the parish church or churches of the bride and the bridegroom. The bishop will dispense from publication for a sufficient cause. In some places the banns for mixed marriages are not called.

3. Notice to be given to Priest

Let this be as long as possible. Three months is not too much, especially where a dispensation has to be obtained. From what has been said it will be clear that it is necessary to give notice to *(a)* the parish priest of the bride; *(b)* the parish priest of the bridegroom (if he lives in another parish), and (c) the parish priest of the church where the marriage is to take place (if different from either *(a)* or *(b)*).

To *(a)* and (b) full names and addresses must be given in order that banns may be published.

Upon the priest who is to attend to the other preliminaries of the marriage—normally *(a)*— both bride and bridegroom should call, although he may wish to speak to them separately. Among the particulars about which he may ask are:—

i. Condition, *i.e.*, bachelor, spinster, widow, or widower.

ii. Certificate of freedom to marry. (This is normally to be obtained from the church where one has been baptised).

iii. Willingness to marry, absence of undue influence on the part of parents or others, etc.

iv. Impediments.

4. *Impediments*

The commonest are:—

i. Consanguinity, or blood relationship. In general it may be said that first or second cousins may not marry without a dispensation, but if the relationship be intricate it may be necessary to prepare a genealogical chart for the priest.

ii. Affinity or relationship by marriage. This cannot occur unless one of the parties has been previously married. In general, we may say that a widow is forbidden, without dispensation, to marry any near blood-relation of her deceased husband, up to and including his first cousins, and vice-versa.

iii. Mixed marriage, *i.e.,* between a Catholic and a baptised non-Catholic. Dispensation for a mixed marriage can only be granted if the two parties give guarantees that all the children, of either sex, shall be baptised in the Catholic Church only and brought up in the Catholic faith, if the non-Catholic party gives a guarantee not to interfere in the free exercise of the faith by the Catholic party, and if there is a moral certainty that these guarantees will be honourably observed. By the ordinary law of charity a Catholic wife or husband is bound to do all that is reasonably possible to promote, by prayer, example, and even, if prudent, by word, the conversion of the non-Catholic partner. For the granting of a dispensation from this or any other impediment a grave reason (or reasons) is required. If there should be question of a marriage between a Catholic and an unbaptised person, the same guarantees as above would be required, but a proportionally graver cause would have to be present.

5. Time of Marriage

Arrange the date and the hour with the priest who is to officiate. If possible, arrange for a Nuptial Mass, which is the normal complement of the marriage ceremony and desired for all her children by the Church. It cannot, however, be celebrated for a mixed marriage, nor during what are called the closed times, *i.e.,* Advent with Christmas Day, and Lent with Easter Sunday.

6. Requirements of the Civil Law

Notice must be given to the Registrar of the district in which the parties live, or to both Registrars if they live in different civil districts. (Note that the civil districts are usually not identical with the Catholic parochial divisions.) Notice of at least three weeks and a day must be given unless the parties are willing to pay for a licence. Arrangements must be made with the Registrar to attend the church on the day and at the hour fixed for the marriage. His attendance may be demanded at the ordinary place of worship of one or both of the parties if it lies within two miles of the furthest limits of the civil district in which notice is given.

COURTSHIP

Hubert McEvoy SJ

COURTSHIP

Hubert McEvoy SJ

The Purpose of Courtship

If, in the Services, it happened that one from every three recruits had soon to be discharged as unfit, responsible officers would doubtless presume that something was wrong with the life, or with the standard of selection, or with the method of training, or with all three. When we are faced with a rapid increase in divorce, when Marriage Guidance Councils have to be set up throughout the country to deal with the number of marriages which are failures, or threaten to become so, one would expect a similar conclusion to be drawn, namely, that something is wrong with the way people view the nature and purpose of marriage, and, consequently, with the way they prepare for marriage during courtship.

A courtship is influenced throughout by how marriage is viewed. It is, then, important to have the right view. Marriage has been called a "total community of life on the mental and spiritual levels". It is, therefore, a great undertaking. A "total community of life" between two people is not lightly to be entered upon. The surrender which it supposes of "exclusive and perpetual rights" over each other is too complete for that. These rights deal with the primary purpose of marriage, the having and training of children, and the value we set on our own life should give us some clue to the nobility and the responsibility of the married state in which husband and wife have it in their power to give life to other human souls, so sharing in the creative work of God and achieving what they could never otherwise do, something eternal, immortal. By training and fashioning the life they give, they share also in the sanctifying work of God. The second purpose of marriage, the "mutual help" of each, means that each sets up a firm barrier against that enemy of many beautiful things, one's selfishness. May it not be that marriage is not to-day sufficiently seen as a noble responsibility embraced and shared by two people? Its nobility is set as high as it possibly could be set, by St Paul when he said of married love that it was to be like that with which "Christ loved the Church."

Courtship, then, is also a noble responsibility. It is the time when it is discovered whether the final responsibility may be safely accepted, whether or not a "total community of life" is possible, whether each can share not only the physical life of the other, but also the mental and spiritual life. It is a seeking for the assurance that the attraction really does come from such a harmony of characters that eventually each may make confidently the surrender of self to the other in marriage. It is for courtship to discover and bring into play the delicate instincts which are in all of us by grace and which are necessary for the nobility and the full happiness of marriage to be realised. Because it is an intimate approach to another human soul, courtship must always be carried on in an atmosphere of delicacy and reverence if these fine instincts, from which alone true love springs, are to be revealed and be seen as part of one's strength for the future.

"Shall I marry?—whom shall I marry?"

The questions may come from new, hardly recognised impulses marking the break-away from the individualism and self-sufficiency of childhood. They indicate the grown-up need to share one's living with another. Feeling oneself to be "in love" should raise another question: "Is it an attraction which will lead to true married love?" Love is a word with many meanings—we speak of loving sport, teaching, gardening, reading—indeed, almost any human activity. Even when we talk of loving people there is a wide variety of meaning. There is the love of friendship, a deep affection for one whose influence both steadies and enriches our own character, and this plays in courtship an important part. But there is also the love of desire, the urge to possess the loved one as one's very own. It differs from the love of friendship—we can share our friends, but not our partners in marriage. These two loves together form the strong natural basis for the lasting union in marriage, which consists in each completely possessing, and being possessed by, the beloved.

If in a courtship there is that feeling that one's character is being steadied and, as it were, added to and strengthened, the love of friendship is leading on to married love, and this suggests that there really is the required compatibility on the mental and spiritual levels. The absence of this, it should be remembered, is even more easily recognised because one is dealing with facts. For instance, on the mental plane, besides possessing the other qualifications for marriage, one partner appreciates good music, has some artistic sense, the other "cares for none of these things," but is limited to the headlines, the comic strip, the fashion or the sporting page, is impatient of any music except that of a stove-pipe band, of any entertainment above the level of the cheap variety.

On the spiritual plane, one may have a conscience that sees the issues between right and wrong quickly and correctly, and a will that decides with little hesitation for the right, whilst the other partner is uncertain in conscience and wavering in will, with a definite inclination to the wrong in such matters as honesty, truth, the lawful use of marriage, and so on. The one does not wish to be merely a Sunday Mass Catholic, but feels the need of a fuller use of the Sacraments and the devotional helps of the Church, finds that Catholic reading helps to maintain a more correct and a happier outlook, considers it a duty to take a reasonable part in Catholic, and particularly in parish, activities; the other may be quite content, and indeed quite good, with doing no more than the Church demands as a minimum.

Mixed Marriages

It is inescapable that a large proportion of mixed marriages are failures and tragedies, proving that the difference of religious outlook does cause serious strain. Religion is an essential part of life. That makes it just as unwise to marry anyone who has little, if any, religious sense as it would be to marry one who preferred a wandering life to a home life. The Catholic partner has to reflect seriously that having grown up in a Catholic atmosphere there is a tendency to take for granted the value of this example. In our Catholic home it is likely that everyone understood why one got up early for Mass and Communion, gave up an entertainment to wait one's turn for Confession, or to attend Benediction, felt it necessary to go to some trouble to keep the laws of fasting and abstinence, to pause and kneel, even when dog-tired, to say one's prayers at night, to be particular about the books one read, the films one saw, the plays one heard, the kind of conversations one carried on, all following out our belief that life was not just a matter of cleverness or good luck, but a matter of co-operation with God. It is quite a different undertaking to keep up these things in married life, deprived of that sympathetic example and opposed, it may be, by definite misunderstanding. Not that the difference of religion is a hopeless difference since many a fine Catholic has grown out of a marriage convert.

It is likely that the partners will be at different levels on all these planes, and yet it is important that each should vary from the other as little as possible, particularly in the matter of religion. It will not do if the weakness of one is beyond the other's strength to inspire and support. It is easy to see that any one of the differences might become a cause of serious conflict when both partners have to adjust themselves, not just during the infrequent hours of courtship, but during the unceasing companionship of married life. Admittedly one does meet husbands and wives of widely differing temperaments who provide excellent foils to each other, as the genial husband is prevented from becoming a gadabout by the tranquillity of a wife who in turn is helped by his cheerfulness not to lapse into over-seriousness.

Training for Marriage

Marriage is rightly called a vocation. That is a state of life as opposed to just a job in life. In spite of a thoroughly bad private life, it is possible to be a successful business man, but it is not possible to be a good father and husband. It is an important point, then, that marriage should be considered as a vocation because it is a freely chosen state of life. Like every other vocation, it has to be decided, and therefore has its period of preparation. Courtship is the noviceship of marriage, serving the double purpose of testing and training. Carried on as a training, it provides, at the same time, the test whether one is meant to marry at all, whether to marry this particular man or woman, whether one is being rightly drawn to some other, or whether the right partner has yet appeared.

Courtship, then, should be seen primarily as a training, but a training with a difference. It cannot be given by others. The two have entered a world which is wonderfully private and intimate, new to themselves and closed to others. Each must help the other, and learn from the other the meaning of this new phase of existence. Turning its opportunities to advantage is the real purpose of courtship. The opportunities for teaching and learning are sure to be there—one may not have had the advantage of a Catholic school, the home may not have been thoroughly Catholic. There may be a wrong attitude to doubtful books, plays, films, a want of reverence for parents (no happy augury for the future home). Here the other partner will bring to bear the finer influence of one's own home. One may have a quarrelsome, easily offended, critical disposition. Here the other partner will show the value of self-control and reasonableness. By showing, for instance, that discussing others freely is not one of his or her faults, there will be created that valuable understanding which should exist between husband and wife, that neither ever discusses the other with anyone at all, not even with one's closest relatives. The Sixth and Ninth Commandments are still more obvious examples of the duty of teaching. Wherever there is a coarse approach, a persistent desire to have what is not lawful, the other will oppose an attitude which by its clear, delicate reverence is bound to make one even more desirable to the partner who is worthy. If it does not, the signal is set at "danger". Faults in courtship are not like those in "rehearsals" which, miraculously, do go right, "on the night". Never delude yourself that it will be all right after marriage. Faults not corrected in courtship will stay. The stronger partner should let it be seen that the continuance of the courtship depends upon definite improvement where weaknesses seem likely to cause unhappiness in the future. All this is even more important where one partner is not a Catholic. A large number of mixed marriages would have been fine Catholic ones if this clear-sighted training had gone on from the start.

Many a novice in a religious order has seemed at first to lack every qualification except goodwill until training gradually discloses the hidden apostle, the future saint. So, many an unsatisfactory character has just been waiting for some good man or woman to do what even his or her parents could not do—bring to bear in courtship the one influence which will be successful. The truth of this is certain: because we "needs must love the highest when we see it", the partner who sets out to be an influence for good is bound to appear so desirable in the eyes of the other that the required improvement is seen as a small price to pay. If the other is unwilling, or not able to pay it, the training has been given, the test has been failed, the courtship should cease, remembering that a wrong marriage is a marriage spoiled, not just for one, but for both.

Each shaping the other for a partnership in which all the virtues and qualities required for a good Catholic life come into action and prove their value—that is surely how happy marriages are made. It is using properly a unique relationship where the influence of one upon the other is at its most powerful. But "no one gives what he does not possess." Courtship should do what every new experience does, bring an awareness, not only of the defects of one's partner, but of one's own. The opportunity is

21

for both and what should be going on is a gradual raising of the level, an enriching of the character through each seeking to be more worthy of the other. The Breviary speaks of the priest as being "increased by the priesthood." Husband and wife should be increased in worth by marriage, and the increase should begin in courtship. Each has to discover whether the one has enough to add to the strength of the other so that life will be fuller and happier for both.

Sex and Emotion

What has been said is of itself almost enough to write off an emotional affair as a failure. Animals respond easily to each other's emotions, but then, they do not have to live together afterwards in the same intimate way that human beings do, and for that, character is needed more than emotion. If the hours of courtship are made just an opportunity for emotional satisfaction, the real purpose, just described, is clearly missed, and it may not be long after marriage that one will ruefully regard the other and think:

"I cannot say

If thou hadst ever met my soul."

It will not be met in an emotional affair. Moreover, there is danger here. The sex impulse which leads men and women to seek life together must, because of what it has to achieve, be a powerful urge. We surround high explosives with all sorts of precautions. God and the Church have surrounded sex, as much because of its sanctity as because of the dangers of its misuse, with clear precautions. Through its associations with the creative activity of God it must be a sacred, beautiful thing and, therefore, more easily spoiled.

The proper training of courtship must produce a marked delicacy and reverence which are the light but powerful hold of the capable rider on the reins of a fine but highly-strung animal ready to tighten at the first sign of panic. In courtship, the reins of delicacy and reverence once slackened, the bounds of lawful intimacies once passed, control is easily lost, and there may be that tragedy, all the sadder because never intended, a painfully regretted betrayal of each other. Couples are often mistaken in thinking they can keep control all along the line just as those who dangerously overwork are convinced they will stop in time before the inevitable breakdown which always takes them by surprise. We must speak about these things, because all too often the good fall into the trap which the less spiritual are cunning enough to avoid.

The girl partner has a special responsibility to remember that sex is usually much more at the alert in the man, and that her seeking a great warmth of affection, which merely gives her innocent pleasure, may involve the other in a serious struggle for self-control, and in painful questionings of conscience. Generally, too, a decent man will not go further than a decent girl wants.

Whenever there is a premature grasping of the privileges of the married state, the feeling that each holds the other in trust is lessened. Each betrays to the other a weakness of will, and there cannot be the same trust and reliance again. The courtship becomes charged with a certain compelling quality which often makes it difficult, if not impossible, to withdraw from a relationship which perhaps is not convincing to either party and which reason tells them should be ended. It is well to be clear-minded, through the guidance of others whom we respect, or of a wise confessor, as to what intimacies are allowed, and when even these are unwise. One must be alone with a person to discover certain aspects of his or her character, but to be alone at certain times or in certain moods may be something more than dangerous. When one knows where the line is drawn for us it is easier to stay on the right side.

If courtship is looked upon as a time when restraint and the practice of doing good to one another brings the reward of an ability to see and appreciate as part of one's own life, the best in each other's character, this will so fill the courtship that the difficulties mentioned in the previous paragraphs will hardly arise. St Augustine says regretfully of the youthful days of himself and his friend, Alypius: "Such honour as there is in marriage and from the duty of well-ordered life together and the having of children had very small influence with either of us." He meant that it should have been the overwhelming influence.

Living Together

"Life together" means innumerable things—what sort of house; how it will be furnished, showily and uselessly, or simply and efficiently; out of income, or by running into debt. If the couple are lucky enough to have a house to go to, there can be hours of useful planning. It is being discovered how much drudgery can be saved by a thoughtfully-planned kitchen. One cannot help feeling that if the husband developed an interest in the house before he lived in it he might not spend so much time out of it. If they have to live with others in the first days of their marriage (and living with in-laws should be a desperate last throw), the planning is even more necessary. In these days of housing shortage, too, the difficulty should not be exaggerated, real as it is. There is more to a home than many rooms and much furniture. Home is not so much a place as an atmosphere. Home is where you are.

> "Thy Kingdom come! Yea, bid it come!
>   But when Thy Kingdom first began
> On earth, Thy Kingdom was a home,
>   A child, a woman, and a man."
>
> (KATHARINE TYNAN)

No mention of rooms, furniture or gardens! There is, too, the standard of one's housekeeping. Some families can live, and be better fed and clothed, at half the cost of others. Even menus might make a pleasant evening for a couple! There can be discussions as to the things that are to be the first charge on one's income, and what provision shall be made for a rainy day, what money the wife is to have, and how far the husband has a right to know about its spending. Frequently recurring "financial embarrassments" destroy the peace of many a family. Even the timetable of the home is worth foreseeing, and making sure that it includes the time for taking each other out, and for going to church, for family prayers, and so on. It is not too early in courtship to discuss children and their training, so that each may learn the other's views and avoid divided counsels afterwards. There are ways in which these discussions can be stimulated by books and pamphlets such as those listed on the covers of this pamphlet. There are sometimes Catholic courses on marriage guidance to be attended. Even the smallest details are worth while. How much trouble would be saved, for instance, if each made a resolve never to discuss the other with anyone at all after marriage.

The last suggestion, however, has an application to courtship. It is certainly worth while to examine fairly hints which others may give, especially if they come from one's own parents, who, whilst they may not know so well the partner of one's choice, do know their own child. This attending to the opinions of others has its value, and those which are inspired by the right intention are soon recognised. It is to-day somewhat necessary. Once, the partners in a courtship usually knew each other from childhood. Now it frequently happens that they have never met before the moment of the first attraction. They have scant knowledge of how each behaves in the home setting, or at what worth they are estimated by others who know them well.

Not All will Marry

It is a mistake to imagine oneself a failure because no partner comes one's way. Not all are meant to be husbands or wives. Some may be fit for marriage but have not met a suitable partner. Others may have to delay marriage because of some other pressing duty which might in circumstances become imperative, such as the care of parents. There are others again who, for reasons of temperament, or some other defect, are unsuited for married life. It is usually a tragedy for such people to marry perforce. Let them realise that they can lead full and happy lives as single men or women. The ranks of social and welfare workers are full of these. They often make great educators, artists, inventors. Freedom from the responsibilities of a family is undoubtedly a great advantage to many and a great benefit to the world.

Some are not meant to marry because God wants them for His own special work, and it does seem that our young

Catholics, girls in particular, are not giving as much thought as they should to the possibility of a religious vocation. Perhaps they are bewildered by the wide range of trades and professions which have been thrown open to them during the last thirty years. It is not at all unlikely that many are leading not very happy lives because a religious vocation was not considered.

But, if it is to be a courtship, let it be so carried on that you can feel that the grace of God is with you in all you do. Each must be able to go on thinking that it has fallen out extremely well that they have met. Nothing should ever be done to destroy that estimate of each other.

> "All other things to their destruction draw,
> Only our love hath no decay;
> This no to-morrow hath, nor yesterday;
> Running it never runs from us away,
> But truly keeps its first, last everlasting day."

GOING STEADY

Tony Kirwin

GOING STEADY

Tony Kirwin

Have you noticed how some adults criticise teenagers because they say they have too much money, too much leisure time and too many worthless things to spend their money on? Frankly, it seems to me that they are a bit jealous. In many ways, I suppose, you can understand it. After all when they were youngsters work, money and leisure time were often hard to come by. You know what they say, 'When I was your age I had 1/6d to last me all week and after work I was too tired to go gallivanting about!' In many cases this was true, but then why do they keep complaining that things have changed for the better? Surely it is much better to thank God for our improved conditions and show our appreciation by making the most of them. I suppose some people are born pessimists.

Enjoying life

Teenagers and the people who work with them, say quite rightly, that leisure time is not wasted time. Teenagers use every minute of it on homework, evening classes, youth clubs, dancing or the cinema. They enjoy life and usually the only time they cease to be happy is when they find themselves at a loose end with nothing to do.

'Getting with it'

And the money, is that wasted? Well you know the answer to that one. The average working teenager pays a very fair share of his earnings into the housekeeping money, he spends a lot on getting to and from work and a lot on keeping clean and smartly dressed. These are the essentials and somehow, thank God, he's still got enough left over to 'get with it' and enjoy his spare time by buying records, a motor cycle or spending weekends camping or mountaineering. More youngsters than ever before are going abroad on holiday, teenagers are in the forefront of campaigns for peace and famine relief. They are amongst the most generous when it comes to giving money or time to good causes.

Teenage idols

The advertising boys and those who peddle the 'popular' forms of 'mass media' have been trying for years to create a 'teenage society'. They've tried to cut a chunk out of the human family so that boys and girls in their teens would feel they were in a class apart from the rest of society. The result has been to make many youngsters feel 'odd' rather than something 'special'.

There's money in it

The high pressure peddlers saw money in teenagers' pockets and decided it would do more good in their own. Like many money-mad people before them they worked on forming a new society, a cult which outwardly flattered its members by 'giving them what they wanted' but which really gave the founders what *they* wanted—cash in the bank.

Success, for whom?

If their only aim was to help young people get the most from life and spend their money wisely, nobody could argue with them. The trouble is they have created an atmosphere of unreality. Listen to the 'pop' songs which tell you, you are never too young to fall in *Love* and seem to be designed to make anyone who isn't going steady by the time they are fifteen feel like a 'queer'. Teenagers say the words don't mean much. True, they don't. But continuous repetition certainly leaves an impression. Look around!

Follow your nose!

Advertisements tell a girl the perfect husband is a man who uses 'after shave', has a new car and an account at so and so's bank. While the perfect girl (significantly, seldom a wife) is desirable, and exciting if she wears so and so's 'bra', uses so and so's perfume and bathes with so and so's soap. Never are human beings good people, kind people, considerate or patient. None of these qualities seem to matter as long as people smell nice and buy lots of things they only want because the advertising men have persuaded them they will be miserable failures without them.

How to succeed

Success and failure do not depend on answering the call of advertisements. There is much more to them than that. Many so-called successful people are in fact failures as *people*, and lead very unhappy lives as a result. Happiness must be counted as part of true success. God wants us to be happy and has made us part of a human family. Our happiness depends on the relationship we establish with the other members of this family. God has given each one of us reason, with emotion and a hundred and one other personal gifts which go to make our individuality. He has also filled the world with good things to help us lead a happy life. We have a duty to use all these things as God intended us to use them. If we misuse God's gifts we stand the chance of committing sin and so making ourselves and others unhappy. Because of our human failings it is sometimes difficult not to misuse the very things which God has designed to make us happy on earth and lead us to even greater happiness in heaven.

We're lucky

The Catholic teenager is luckier than others. He knows that he can bring God into everything so that if temptation comes along he need never face it alone. He knows that if he trusts God, and uses the graces He has provided, he will be able to get the most out of life all along the line. We all have a common desire to be happy and being happy is the greatest compliment we can pay to God. Happiness is a personal thing but it comes with sharing our life with God and our fellow human beings in an unselfish way.

You have probably already thought of the day when you will share your life completely with a member of the opposite sex. Let's take a look at this road to happiness and see how we can be true partners in God's plan for the world.

BOY MEETS GIRL

Until your early teens you probably haven't bothered much with the opposite sex. Possibly even now you are not particularly interested in them and prefer the company of friends of your own sex. This is quite normal. Some people are just naturally not attracted to the other sex for a much longer period than others. In any case friends of either sex will always be, it is hoped, an important part of your life.

A worth-while technique

All the time you are growing physically the need to express physical attraction for others is growing within you too.

Sooner or later a young man starts looking for his 'dream girl'. His first approaches are probably either too boisterous or too shy to do anything other than amuse, and secretly flatter, the girl. Later, and probably many girls later, he will be more at ease and natural. Every young man has to learn how to be at ease in feminine company. Like any worth-while technique it takes time to learn. A boy shouldn't be too envious of the chap who can 'slay 'em at a glance'. He, too, has his problems.

A girl probably starts looking for her 'prince charming' a little earlier but she, too, goes through a 'silly stage'. She want boys to notice her but makes things a bit too obvious. She giggles and teases and the poor lad just can't stand the pace. He retreats back to the company of his male gang. But she has learned a lesson. Next time he will not want to leave so quickly.

Puzzled

The boy and girl are experiencing new feelings, new emotions because their bodies are still growing towards adulthood. Each should show great consideration for the other's feelings. They may just want a good time together and do not intend to marry. Fair enough. But all they do together, all the considerations they show for each other's feelings and failings will one day be related to the partner they eventually marry.

Confidence

Gradually boy and girl find out what makes the other tick. Sometimes they are in time with each other, sometimes they are not. They have reached the stage of being able to seek the other's hand and know the sheer joy of that hand not being withdrawn, felt the wonderful, tender clasp that means two people want to share affections. Suddenly there is a new reason for living. Does the world drag when they're apart and fly when they're together? Does it stop completely? Who knows? Only them. Who cares? Only them. They know what champagne feels like, full of effervescence and longing to be consumed. Yet, somewhere they've read that champagne improves with keeping, if it's kept in the bottle at the right temperature.

A time for honesty

This is a most important time, a preparation for marriage. Each will have to decide, 'Is this for keeps?' 'Could I stand the other's faults until death do us part?' Great honesty is required in the pictures they draw of each other. If those nagging little habits and imperfections can't be curbed then they must be admitted and looked at squarely. Are they serious enough to ruin a marriage? Are they just amusing little things which somehow make the other what they are, and add the colour to their personality?

Sex is ceasing to be the dirty word they used to think it was when they were younger. It is starting to have a meaning it didn't have before. They realise that sex is a power within them which will have wonderful possibilities. Any young couple who look eagerly to a future together must begin to realise that sex is good, that if they use it properly they will have something like God's power to create. They can be partners with God in His plan for the world. Because of this, sex is something sacred which mustn't be misused or degraded. God made the Sacrament of Holy Matrimony so that men and women can use their sexual powers in security and freedom.

Why marry?

Like everything God made, He made sex for a purpose. He made it to ensure the future of the human race. Man and woman would be attracted to each other so that in their company His plan could continue. Like all His gifts it was to be enjoyed, not just for a brief moment that left behind a store of frustrations, unhappiness and doubt, but a lasting pleasure which would enrich the people concerned in a way that is impossible in any other. The only way to ensure this was to make their relationship permanent. Marriage made sense of the sexual act. With marriage children would be welcomed because they were an extra part of two people who loved each other enough to want to stay together for a lifetime. Here was security for man, wife and children. They all had a common bond of love. Marriage made children the logical outcome of their parents' union. They were something more of each other to love.

A miracle

So important is it for children to be born to a marriage that God has made man much more sexually sensitive than the woman. It is as though man must always be prepared to share himself with his wife so that God's plan for the world can continue and the miracle of conception and birth take place.

Before marriage

A girl would do well to realise that the handsome, curly haired boy who makes her tingle from head to toe with femininity and feel like a goddess, is really a power-house of sexual activity who is only stopped from turning his fantasies into reality by respect for her feminine person. Should she cheapen her femininity, or allow it to be cheapened, and so destroy his respect, she must share the blame for the consequences.

What's the motive?

Prince Charming's desires are easily aroused. All five senses and his imagination as well can send sensual stimuli racing through his system and quickly become localised in his sexual organs. This is how it should be. This is how God made him, so that in marriage he would be the dominant partner. But, as a single man it means he must keep a pretty firm hold on his power of self control.

He takes a far less romantic view of courting and marriage than does his 'dream girl'. She enjoys the feeling of being wanted, of being someone special. She dreams of the wedding, her future home and her 'man about the house'. A boy thinks far more about the sexual aspects of their relationship whereas the girl takes a more tender and romantic view of love. In marriage their emotions will mingle. The girl won't have a monopoly of tenderness and the sexual aspect, too, will mean a great deal to her.

How far can you go?

Every young person thinking about marriage obviously knows of the other's common desire for fulfilment but it is important to realise that basically the initial motives are different. Because of these differences you must be careful during your courting days. As friends you will want to share things, buy each other gifts, go to the cinema and dancing. You will also want to kiss and enjoy physical contact. How far can you go? What is the answer? Think for a while over what you know. 1. Sexual intercourse is to take place only between man and wife. 2. God wants you to be happy and enjoy your youth.

Remember these two things and the answer comes naturally. Don't allow yourselves to be so aroused that there is a danger that you will not be able to stop yourselves acting like man and wife, when in fact you are not man and wife. You are young and happy and nothing should interfere with this. You cannot be happy if you force others to do your wishes, nor if the result of your pleasures bring unhappiness to others.

In short, if either of you feel the need for the sexual intercourse you are not entitled to, you must put the brakes on immediately.

Semen should only leave a man's body unconsciously during sleep or during sexual intercourse with his wife. Try not to put yourselves in a situation where this is likely to happen at any other time.

Love

You love each other, you want each other, but love doesn't start, nor end in sexual intercourse. It is a growing thing which starts when you are first aware of each other as persons, and continues growing all through marriage. At different times, different aspects of your love will have to show themselves. It is an exciting game of challenge and discovery with all the dignity of a God-made emotion. We know that God is Love and in loving Him and others we are doing what He most wants us to do. Physical love is an important part of Gods plan but it must be played according to the rules if it is not to be selfish and inconsiderate. It is the way in which husband and wife become father and mother and establish a relationship which is so deep that their very personalities as well as their bodies become fulfilled and enriched. It is an intimate and sacred involvement which can withstand any attempts to degrade it.

What people say

Many well-meaning people try to advise young people not to have sexual intercourse before marriage, by saying such things as, 'Think of the child which may be born and the worry you'll cause to your poor parents!' They usually add something about the risks of catching V.D., too! These are valid reasons, perhaps, but they are not ones which would spring to mind when the passions run high. No, the unmarrieds' only way to keep their courtship holy is by deciding to accept, right from the start, God's wish that they should fulfil their desires only in marriage and so provide security for His children and themselves. This means that they decide on a code of conduct, compatible with their own personalities, so that nothing is likely to happen which will make them less than the real and reasoning man and woman they hope they are. It requires great self control and this is not easy unless we practise it on smaller things beforehand.

We are all God's children and He has given us a legacy of graces which we can draw on through the sacraments and prayer. Without these helping hands from God it is often very difficult to make the right decisions. They can motivate us in the right directions so that we get the most from life and they can help to stop us should we take the wrong road in a moment of weakness. You can't expect to make an emergency stop if you've never used the brakes before. Keep them in good trim and watch for the warning signals. Jump the lights and anything could happen.

At large in the world

When you were children you accepted the standards you were being taught without question. You were shielded from many of the unpleasant things which were happening around you. When you left school you started to see the world in a different way. Many people professed to have high moral standards but in fact lived a lie. You met people who disregarded honesty and would do anything for a 'quick buck'. You had been taught that the human body was sacred and yet in magazines, films and in the street you saw it degraded, sold for cash or brutalised for pleasure. Your Faith was something you loved and yet people needed little excuse to mock the most sacred things.

You must decide

Are there such things as right and wrong or is the adult world just every man for himself? You've a big decision to make. Balance what you have been taught is right and good against what others are doing with their lives. Remember that the Church has only survived because it was founded by God to help people to love Him and their fellow men and show them the way to everlasting life. Love is truth. All through history men, women, boys and girls have died defending this truth. Without it their lives would have been nothing. With it even their deaths were the start of a wonderful new life.

Every day in the newspapers we are given new, terrifying statistics about crime, suicides, divorces, unmarried mothers and such like. When standards fall, these statistics rise. Many of our fellow human beings are lost and confused and we must pray for them and help them. Remember our Faith is a rock that does not change its eternal truths. Stick by it and our lives will have wonderful stability.

The Church is a family and like a united human family it is able to give it's members security and a feeling of being wanted. The Church has a timeless quality, too, because of the wonderful unity between its members in heaven and its members on earth. The saints are our brothers and sisters and will help us at any time we care to ask. Christ has given us priests to look after His family on earth and we should remember that they are always willing to advise us on life's problems. They are men with a very real experience of life. They have spent years in training and years in helping people. Never feel that your problems are too great or too slight to tell a priest. He wants to help you because in being of service to you he is fulfilling his vocation, being the father God has wished him to be to His children.

SEX EDUCATION: TRAINING IN CHASTITY

Malcolm Brennan

SEX EDUCATION

Training in Chastity

Malcolm Brennan

Sex education is, or ought to be, training in chastity. If a sex education course is not primarily training in chastity, then it ought to be labelled what it is: biology, or hygiene or population studies, or whatever. If such a course purports to tell the purpose, the meaning, or the human values in its subject, but is not geared both immediately and ultimately to the advancement of chastity, it is a fraud. An unconscious fraud, or an invincibly ignorant one, perhaps, but still a fraud.

I. What Sex Is For

Words, like fashions, have a way of popping into popularity and fading out again; and since chastity is not now one of the livelier topics of conversation, it might be a good idea to pause and introduce ourselves to it again, and to its neighbours purity, decency, modesty, and virginity. Theologians define chastity as the moral virtue by which people regulate and moderate their sexual drives. It is one of a family of virtues called temperance, which helps us to moderate and regulate all our instincts and emotions – our impulses toward food, comfort, safety, sex, anger, fear, hatred, pity, and the like. It is rather curious that in the case of many of these there is a name for the sin involved (like gluttony) but not for the corresponding virtue; yet in the case of sex there is the sin of lust and the virtue of chastity. The practice of chastity then, is the practice of temperance in matters of sex.

And temperance? It has to do with modulation and seasonableness, with exercising our various capacities in right measure, in due proportion, at the proper time, for a fitting purpose, and in harmony with our whole person.

Of the four neighbours of chastity mentioned above – purity, decency, modesty, and virginity – the first two usually refer, often without much precision, to sexual attitudes as a personal mental state (purity), and to sexual behaviour in its social dimensions (decency). With more precision, modesty is the practice of chastity with respect to sexual display, and virginity as a moral virtue is the most excellent form of chastity, the forgoing of the use of sex faculties for the love of God.

Chastity, then, once again, is the moral virtue by which men and women moderate and regulate their sexual emotions and instincts. But having sorted out chastity in this way, we still have not got to the heart of the matter. The most indulgent sensualist recognizes the practical need to moderate and regulate his indulgence, if only to savour the delights more fully. Is this chastity? Hardly, because the whole sense and meaning of chastity both in its broadest outlines and in its minutest details depends upon what sex is for. If its purpose is to provide pleasure, then our sensualist is right in regulating to maximize his thrills. If its purpose is to provide an optimum balance between workers and consumers in an industrialized world, then governments are right to control the reproduction of citizens. If our sexual faculties are given us as a means of self-realization or as a way of giving pleasure to others, then we are free to indulge or refrain as particular circumstances seem to offer promising opportunities.

Whatever smattering of truth there may be in those popular attitudes, the Church confidently assures us what it is really for: to people heaven.

Each person is brought into existence, through the coupling of a man and a woman, so that he may participate in God's glory, here in the life of grace and hereafter in ineffable beatitude. Sex is, of course, many things to many people — anything so closely tied up with creation, providence and human nature is bound to be of stupendous proportions, with many dimensions eluding our ready grasp. But men still agree (they may not for long) in calling sex a reproduction system, not a recreation system or a communication system. Whatever particular worthy or unworthy intentions people bring to the use of sex — loving surrender, aggressive conquest, the sale of toothpaste — it is obvious that the discrete components fit together to constitute a system that reproduces, that makes new people. And people are for God. And however perfectly or imperfectly people who use sex are able to conform their wills to God's generous design, and whatever the grand or not-so-grand purposes they might have besides, the Church insists that they must not thwart God's holy method of making people for his love.

But more than some minimum participation in God's plan, advocates of chastity ought to celebrate the splendours of that family loving which conforms fully, generously, and openly to the Father's love. Concerned young people looking for daring critiques of the state of the world and bold programmes for its rescue should be able to find their dreams come true in the

Church's teaching on sex and its right use, for it is at once truly cosmic and deeply personal. As God apparently filled the vast celestial reaches with multitudes of the heavenly host all in a moment, so he might have created the whole human race in another moment. But he chose otherwise. He directly created only two human beings to start with 'and male and female he created them', and he chose to rely upon their sexual intercourse to complete his mighty work of creation.

Why God should have arranged matters in this startling way is beyond me – some unfathomable mystery of divine condescension. But it is not unique, it fits a pattern. He chose to effect our redemption not by some exquisitely remote divine operation but by getting himself born of a woman and nailed to a cross; he has chosen to use plain water in washing away our original sin; he feeds our immortal souls with the commonest food, bread; and he prepares them for entrance into his august presence with, of all things, olive oil. All these wonders, and more, we are familiar with under the rather austere term, sacramental system.

And marriage is a sacrament. As if the natural purpose of reproduction – the procreation of persons for heaven – were not enough, he has gone one better and made it a special means of grace, the divine life within us. That is to say, just as God has chosen water, and bread, and olive oil, and verbal formulas, and other such commonplaces, to effect our rescue, so has he also chosen human sexuality.

It has been disconcerting to some (Manicheans and Jansenists – our Catholic brand of puritans) that God should tie himself down, as it were, to sexual intercourse, and not only to that in the blessed marriage bed but also to the promiscuous, the adulterous, the rapacious (but not the contracepted, in marriage or out). But the Church continues to preach this high destiny for sex, this double destiny of making people, and making people holy – of procreating human beings for God's glory, and of sanctifying them through matrimony for sharing in that glory.

These are the stupendous facts of life that must soak through the minds and hearts of us parents, pastors, and teachers who are charged with telling about sex, whether explaining in the simplest terms where the new kitties came from or whether making advanced studies of DNA. And, unlike some of what follows, these teachings of the Church are indisputably clear: people ought to be encouraged in the practice of chastity; chastity is the right use of sex, sex is God's instrument for peopling heaven.

II. Signs Of The Times

Many years ago during the golden age (whenever that was) people lived in Catholic cultures and on farms. There they learned from the cows and the corn, with no traumatic fanfare, what reproduction was all about on the natural level; and from their now quaint customs of courtship and marriage they learned its meaning on the human level; and from their lively faith they learned its spiritual dimensions. But nowadays children learn that bread comes from the supermarket, animals from the zoo or pet shop, and babies from a hospital or a terrible mistake. Is there any hope of recreating those golden conditions in the modern world? Well, only a fool would see the prospects as very bright – and perhaps only a fool would raise the question in the first place. But if it is true, as all agree, that conditions in the modern world do not encourage chastity, then surely we who do encourage it must make it our business to try to understand these conditions, to become alert critics of society and, where possible, reformers of it. We should try to understand what the automobile has done to courtship, for example, or what increased longevity is doing to the family, or how property and tax laws affect the establishment of homes. Few of us can become expert in these difficult matters, of course, but all of us have the duty of reading the signs of the times, as Vatican II emphasized. For an important part of training in chastity is the identification and encouragement of good customs (like mothers nursing their infants) and the discouragement of bad ones (like steady dating by those who are years away from marriage).

A dangerous duty in this connection is the necessity of placing the Church's teaching in the modern idiom. This is the problem of putting the ancient revealed truth in terms that men use today – in psychological terms, for example. The man who thinks of the inner life in terms of id, super ego, complex, neurosis, and the like, is usually baffled and often angered by talk about soul, sacramental character, grace, spirit, and the rest of that splendid vocabulary that Scripture and Catholic tradition have given us. To him it is like talking about medicine in terms of herbs, simples, vapours, and leeches. Nor is this a problem for experts only: each of us must similarly try to translate the language of films, beauty contests, the press, politicians – for these and many more sources are continually moulding the thinking of our charges (and ourselves). The reason this project is dangerous is that too often the new language just cannot carry the weight of divine revelation. When we translate 'It is better to give than to receive' into modern terms, 'It is better to be a producer than a consumer', we can congratulate ourselves on speaking the language that men understand today and thereby getting a hearing for the Gospel that it would not have had; but we should not be so smug as to forget that we have confined the precept to economic activities by that language, and we have also lost the 'give', the generosity, of the Biblical form.

And the constant danger is that we will be satisfied to tell only so much of revelation as will fit into the language of economics, or psychology (in talking about love), or sociology (in talking about courtship and marriage), or the language of popular films, or political campaigns, or advice-to-the-lovelorn columns – depending on the interests of our charges. The habit of the sacred writers is instructive: they do not think of themselves as talking about God 'in other words', but rather as proclaiming and spreading the word of God.

We all recognize the danger that pornography poses to chastity, especially in adolescents. But there is a subtler danger, more pervasive and more difficult to combat. It is that syndrome of attitudes and values which we may call, for want of a better name, romantic love. (See how obscure it is? We do not even know what to call it.) It is that fantastic array of some truths, more half-truths, and mostly utter nonsense about love, that finds expression in notions like these: one falls in love, or out, and is powerless to control this love; it is an exquisite emotion which no one can explain; only people who are truly in love should get married, and conversely, people who are truly in love need not bother to get married; love brings happiness and contentment (if it does not, it must not have been true love); when love cools, it is hypocrisy for former lovers to remain together; nothing must stand in the way of love – money, society, family, children; and so on almost forever. Romantic love saturates not only thousands of bad novels, films, and songs, but also many quite good ones. It was introduced into

Western culture in about the eleventh century by troubadours, who picked it up from the Arabs, and it has dug itself in deeply in the nearly thousand years since. It is no easy task to sort out and identify its pernicious influence on ourselves, much less on the young.

Another major difficulty in promoting a right understanding and right use of sex (i.e. chastity) is the bafflingly complex nature of sex. The intricacies of biological reproduction have amazed the modern scientific world since Mendel (an Augustinian monk) began to formulate the laws of genetics over a century ago. Psychology has described a maze of sexual drives and a wonderland of the contortions they undergo. Social sciences too, like politics and anthropology, and the arts as well, seem to be showing a new awareness of the multifarious complexities and extensiveness of sex. What these arts and sciences have discovered seems to be fundamentally this, that men and women are masculine and feminine through and through, not just in their reproductive organs. (Of course, our ancestors knew this from the beginning, and accordingly assigned male and female roles domestically, economically, socially, politically, etc; but somehow there is a difference when modern men discover the same thing by modern methods.)

Nor have theologians been laggard in this regard. There is the problem of modesty – sexual display – for example. Sexual display is a means of invitation to intercourse and therefore should never be used except with one's spouse. But how can people suppress their sexuality, their masculinity or femininity? It shows in their beard or beardlessness, in the quality of their voices, in the shape of their fingernails. The solution of some modern theologians is to introduce a distinction: there is genital sexuality (having to do directly with reproduction), then there is generic sexuality (having to do with masculinity and femininity in a general way – as in voice, beard, and the like).

No doubt a useful distinction. But it too has pitfalls. It tends to divide a person up into disconnected parts. For example, a woman's hands are only generically sexual, not genitally so; thus she can decorate her hands till they look like small chandeliers with no regard to modesty. Something is wrong with this, something that popular language recognized a few years ago in the extensive use of the adjective 'sexy' when it was applied to sexy hands, sexy teeth, sexy shoes, even sexy automobiles.

And the Catholic habit of thought, as the popular, would seem to lead one to search for wholeness, integrity – not to leave, for example, feminine possessiveness and masculine dominance as isolated curiosities of human nature unrelated to God's grand design when male and female he created us. It is probably not the genital sexuality alone that God uses in producing people for heaven, but probably the whole range of sexual differences. Perhaps in this case male dominance and female possessiveness, if chastely exercised, provide something like the vertical and the horizontal axes of family life, and their point of intersection is the centre of the family circle, the one drawing the family members together (female), and the other providing direction for growth (male). And perhaps this dominance and possessiveness, if exercised unchastely, are nothing but the masculine and feminine forms of selfishness.

Not only the habit of Catholic thinking tends in this direction along with popular speech. Science demonstrates over and over again the intimate, if still mysterious, connections between apparently unrelated parts of ourselves, especially of women. The birth-control pill alone has shown that tampering with genital functions produces all sorts of unexpected results in women's other feminine features, their hair, complexion, equanimity, weight, nails, and so on. And before you know it, somebody is going to figure out how femininity is connected with the moon. All of which is to say that we are male and female to the core, and that chastity, therefore, is a function of nearly every part of us – chastity being the moderation and regulation of our male and female drives.

III. Recent Church Guidance

In the face of these puzzles and anomalies and downright threats, what are we to do, we who are charged by God with the promotion of chastity? We have seen the basic doctrine of the Church regarding procreation and the sacrament of marriage. In addition to that, recent Popes have provided three clear principles regarding the instruction of the young in matters of sex.

One is that the primary responsibility, for sex as for other education, rests upon parents – a principle, alas, almost as widely repeated as it is violated. Back in that golden age when the village priest taught catechism to a dozen children, life was simple: what he had to teach was clear, and he knew each child's family. But nowadays a teacher faces thirty more or less anonymous children, and is guided by twice that many agencies – echelons of education committees and sub-committees, task forces of text-book promoters, then the deanery and diocesan and regional and national commissions and their voluminous reports, and also this month's crop of experts with their revolutionary findings. As the bureaucracy takes over more and more of sex education, parents – and pastors, too – have less and less chance to get a word in edgewise. It is even worse when some educators, reversing the order of nature, use children by placing on them the burden of educating their parents in the latest batch of bright ideas. Yet, however glum the prospects of its ever being generally practised, the principle is nevertheless clear: in educating children about sex, chastity, and everything, a child's parents outrank everyone else in the world. They do not have this right because of their greater knowledge or love, or because democracies concede this liberty to their citizens. Rather they have it because of – are you ready? – because of their sex, their genes, their blood in his veins, their maternity and paternity. Teachers are no doubt fine people and very clever and badly put upon (I'm one myself), but they do not make people for heaven as parents do, and especially they do not receive sacramental graces to educate children as parents and those in orders do. And if there is no sacrament for teachers, much less is there one for directors, and executive secretaries, and commissioners.

Another clear declaration of recent Pontiff's is that the more intimate aspects of sex should be taught in private. One sometimes hears the objection, 'There is nothing dirty about sex, and treating it secretively gives children an unwholesome attitude.' A glib objection, and superficial. Modesty is not some new invention alien to human nature, nor a superstitious relic from a benighted past. Shame and modesty may be part of a human nature which is fallen, as Adam and Eve discovered to their chagrin, but it is the only human nature that we have. Teaching children, by word or example, to live without shame or modesty is teaching them to live like angels, or animals.

A third clear teaching of the Church through recent Popes is that children should be taught only as much about sex as they require, lest salaciousness be advanced instead of chastity. The danger is peculiar to sex: one may teach about anger, theft, selfishness, and many other things with little danger of making students angry, thieving, or selfish. But talk about sex and lust can make them feel sexy and lustful. 'Only as much'... it is a charge from the Church that demands our utmost prudence. One Catholic expert (H. V. Slatter, 'Sex Education', in *The New Catholic Encyclopedia*) opines, with many stipulations and precautions about particular circumstances and individual differences, that girls by the age of twelve and boys by the age of thirteen should have a true, but not too detailed, knowledge of: (1) the extent of bodily differences between the sexes; (2) the idea of pregnancy and birth; (3) the physical changes in themselves (emission and menstruation); (4) the meaning of sexual passion; and (5) the fact of sexual intercourse.

'Only as much' does not mean that information should be confined only to the immediate physical facts a child is curious about, and nothing else. On the contrary, the 'else' should always be placed first, that is, God's role for sex in his creative plan, and the 'facts' limited to those the child can properly appreciate. For example, if a young child asks why his mother has breasts, he should be told that God provides them for feeding the baby (absolutely true, no falsehood), but he should certainly not be burdened with information about the breast as an erogenous zone (which married couples, by the way, should learn about as part of the grand design for peopling the kingdom of God).

Finally, the latest guidance from Rome is the most hopeful. Pope Paul has boldy invited us to re-examine the person of Mary and the cults in her honour. (See *To Honour Mary*, CTS Do 462.) Centuries ago, when the troubadours introduced new ideas about women in their romantic love songs, ideas which threatened morality, chivalry, the family, and a good bit else, the response of the Church was to turn to Mary to find out what women are supposed to be and to test those new ideas against her. To our ancestors who cherished the delicately beautiful feudal lady and her devoted knight, the Church showed our Lady, and it devised those Marian devotions which still enrich our spirits.

Analyses of woman based on sociology, biology, psychology, economics, politics, aesthetics, and the whole battery of modern knowledge must proceed apace, and Catholics are not only duty bound but privileged to pursue the principles and findings of those arts and sciences as far as humanly possible. But a sense of the Faith tells us that we can only know the truth in the new ideas by testing them against, not a principle or technique, but a person, Mary. And as of yore the whole body of the faithful turned to Mary as by an infallible instinct of the people of God, so now we are invited to enter this exciting enterprise on our own, to find out Mary for ourselves, not waiting for a theological commission to come up with the answers.

That is fine for women, you say, for Mary is the model of femininity; but what about men, the big shots of this world? Well, men are always chasing off after their dragons, or their South Sea Bubbles, or their Professional Success, but the thing that really keeps the world going (i.e. continuing to people heaven) is how those men return home to their womenfolk. And men's attitudes toward women – again, a sense of the Faith tells us – are best defined in their attitudes toward Mary. She manages somehow to be, all at once, our majestic queen, our most compassionate mother (when those dragons and

Professions turn on us), a mother for our children (in whose care they are safer than in our own), and our delicate sister who needs our manly protection.

BACKGROUND

The anonymous *Courtship* of 1936 is brisk and practical; it only descends to technicality in its appendix on the practical, legal business of marriage (banns, impediments, registrars and so on).

Hubert McEvoy's 1951 text, on the other hand, is wordier, more theoretical, and conveys an idealized picture of marriage and courtship. It is notably light on practical detail. Nevertheless it was frequently reprinted until the early 1970s; only the cover picture was updated.

Tony Kirwin's *Going Steady* of 1964 is a very different text. It takes self-conscious aim at older teenagers and, although much of its language and assumptions have dated, it is not afraid to be clear where its predecessors were intentionally vague.

Brennan's 1974 *Sex Education* is aimed not at young people but at parents, catechists, teachers and whoever else has the unenviable task of trying to convince them of the value of chastity. It recasts traditional teaching in contemporary language.

CTS ONEFIFTIES

1. **FR DAMIEN & WHERE ALL ROADS LEAD** · *Robert Louis Stevenson & G K Chesterton*
2. **THE UNENDING CONFLICT** · *Hilaire Belloc*
3. **CHRIST UPON THE WATERS** · *John Henry Newman*
4. **DEATH & RESURRECTION** · *Leonard Cheshire VC & Bede Jarrett OP*
5. **THE DAY THE BOMB FELL** · *Johannes Siemes SJ & Bruce Kent*
6. **MIRACLES** · *Ronald Knox*
7. **A CITY SET ON A HILL** · *Robert Hugh Benson*
8. **FINDING THE WAY BACK** · *Francis Ripley*
9. **THE GUNPOWDER PLOT** · *Herbert Thurston SJ*
10. **NUNS – WHAT ARE THEY FOR?** · *Maria Boulding OSB, Bruno Webb OSB & Jean Cardinal Daniélou SJ*
11. **ISLAM, BRITAIN & THE GOSPEL** · *John Coonan, William Burridge & John Wijngaards*
12. **STORIES OF THE GREAT WAR** · *Eileen Boland*
13. **LIFE WITHIN US** · *Caryll Houselander, Delia Smith & Herbert Fincham*
14. **INSIDE COMMUNISM** · *Douglas Hyde*
15. **COURTSHIP: SOME PRACTICAL ADVICE** · *Anon, Hubert McEvoy SJ, Tony Kirwin & Malcolm Brennan*
16. **RESURRECTION** · *Vincent McNabb OP & B C Butler OSB*
17. **TWO CONVERSION STORIES** · *James Britten & Ronald Knox*
18. **MEDIEVAL CHRISTIANITY** · *Christopher Dawson*
19. **A LIBRARY OF TALES – VOL 1** · *Lady Herbert of Lea*
20. **A LIBRARY OF TALES – VOL 2** · *Eveline Cole & E Kielty*
21. **WAR AT HOME AND AT THE FRONT** · *"A Chaplain" & Mrs Blundell of Crosby*
22. **THE CHURCH & THE MODERN AGE** · *Christopher Hollis*
23. **THE PRAYER OF ST THÉRÈSE OF LISIEUX** · *Vernon Johnson*
24. **THE PROBLEM OF EVIL** · *Martin D'Arcy SJ*
25. **WHO IS ST JOSEPH?** · *Herbert Cardinal Vaughan*